QUICK Affirmations FOR CHILDREN

A TO Z OF EASY MOTIVATIONS
FOR CREATING BETTER DAYS

Be well + kind to yourself!
xoxo
Kim Ann

Copyright © 2022

Quick Affirmations for Children

ISBN 978-1-953774-30-9 Paperback
ISBN 978-1-953774-32-3 Digital

Published by Lucky Four Press, LLC, 2022

Printed in the USA. All rights reserved.
No part of this book may be reproduced in any form without the written permission of the copyright holders.

All inquiries including bulk purchases for promotional, educational, and business events, should be directed to:

Lucky Four Press, LLC.
9121 Atlanta Ave, Ste 1019
Huntington Beach, CA 92646
www.luckyfourpress.com

This book belongs to:
_____

To Ma,

Thank you for always listening to my ideas and believing in me. You taught me the power of being optimistic, no matter the circumstance.

Your positivity has inspired me to chase my biggest dreams!

Love, Yobe

Quick Affirmations for Children

Let's learn ABC affirmations!

Sometimes, you might not feel brave or confident. That's okay. But it's important that you know how special you are. Focus on the good things in your life. Smile! And remember that you are amazing.

Affirmations can help you feel happier. They can remind you that you are kind, clever, and unique. They can help you feel stronger and more confident.

That's why we wrote this ABC affirmation book! This book is designed to help you do your best and reach for the stars.

Read this book every day. Say the affirmations out loud. You are amazing, brilliant, and confident! You can achieve your dreams. When you believe in yourself, anything is possible.

We can't wait for this book to help you feel more positive!

Happy reading!

Yobe G Kim

I am **confident** in my **choices**.
I'm in **charge** of ME!

I am
destined
for greatness and
deserving
of love!

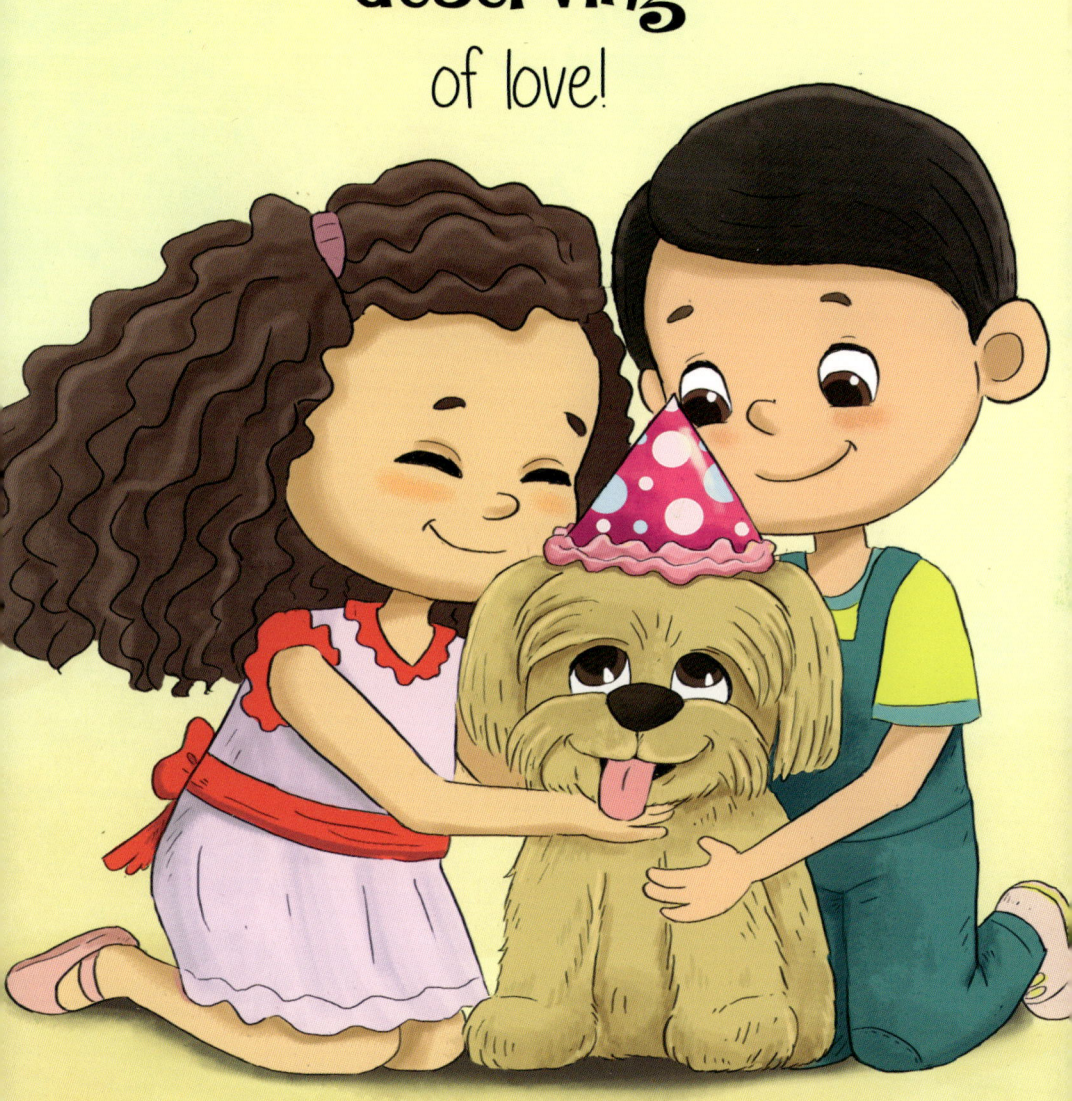

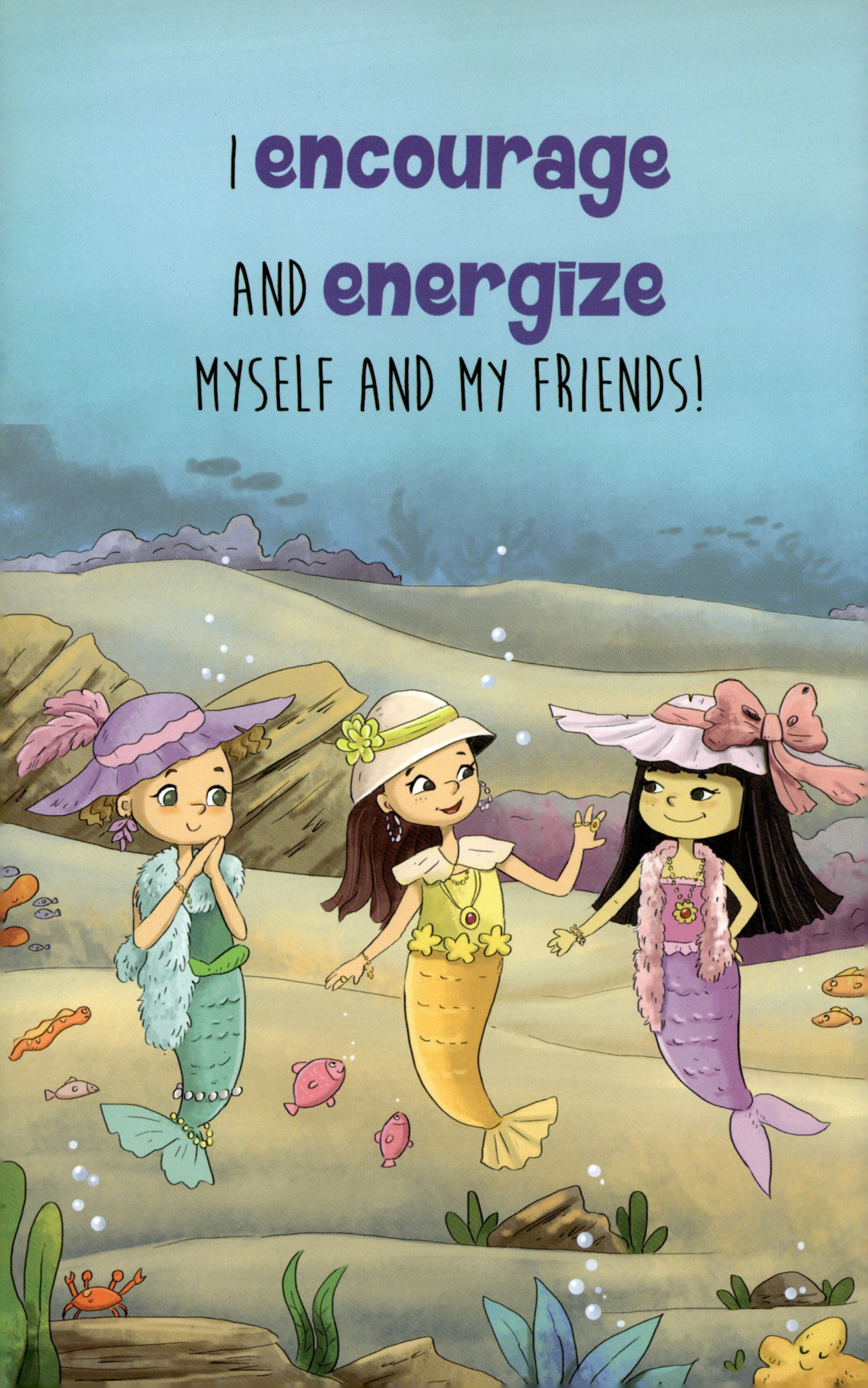

I am **helpful** to others!

I AM **KIND** TO MYSELF
AND
KIND TO OTHERS!

I AM **LOVED** BY MANY!

I am *mindful* of the world around me!

I am necessary and needed!

I am
ONE-OF-A-KIND,
and I am
OPEN-MINDED!

I am **PROUD** of who I am and what I can do!

I ask important and necessary

questions!

I have *respect* for myself and others!

I am
smart,
and I will be
successful!

I am trustworthy and thoughtful!

I am WONDERFUL and WORTHY!

I send hugs and kisses
XOXO
to my family, my friends,
and the whole world!

Yes!
I can make a difference!

I am Zen
and I can find peace!

Affirmations

Affirmations

Affirmations

Affirmations